# The ANIMALS NOAH FORGOT

A.B Paterson

Illustrated by Norman Lindsay

**Angus&Robertson**
An imprint of HarperCollins*Publishers*

AN ANGUS & ROBERTSON BOOK
An imprint of HarperCollinsPublishers

First published in 1933
This edition first published in Australia by Angus & Robertson Publishers in 1990
Reprinted in 1992
CollinsAngus&Robertson Publishers Pty Limited (ACN 009 913 517)
A division of HarperCollinsPublishers (Australia) Pty Limited
25–31 Ryde Road, Pymble NSW 2073, Australia

HarperCollinsPublishers (New Zealand) Limited
31 View Road, Glenfield, Auckland 10, New Zealand

HarperCollinsPublishers Limited
77– 85 Fulham Palace Road, London W6 8JB, United Kingdom

Poetry by A. B. Paterson: copyright Retusa Pty Ltd 1933, 1990
Illustrations by Norman Lindsay : copyright Janet Glad 1933, 1990

National Library of Australia
Cataloguing-in-Publication data:

Paterson, A. B. (Andrew Barton), 1864–1941.
    The animals Noah Forgot
    ISBN 0 207 16194 1.

    1. Animals — Juvenile poetry. 2. Children's poetry,
    Australian. I. Lindsay, Norman, 1879–1969. II. Title.
A821'.2

Designed by Christie & Eckermann
Illustrations hand-coloured for this edition by Karen Ball
Typeset by Midland Typesetters, Victoria
Printed in Hong Kong

5  4  3  2
95  94  93  92

# CONTENTS

# Prologue

## AUSTRALIAN SCENERY

*The Mountains*

A land of sombre, silent hills, where mountain cattle go
By twisted tracks, on sidelings steep, where giant gumtrees grow
And the wind replies, in the river oaks, to the song of the stream below.

A land where the hills keep watch and ward, silent and wide awake
As those who sit by a dead campfire, and wait for the dawn to break,
Or those who watched by the Holy Cross for the dead Redeemer's sake.

A land where silence lies so deep that sound itself is dead
And a gaunt grey bird, like a homeless soul, drifts, noiseless, overhead
And the world's great story is left untold, and the message is left unsaid.

## *The Plains*

A land, as far as the eye can see, where the waving grasses grow
Or the plains are blackened and burnt and bare, where the false mirages go
Like shifting symbols of hope deferred — land where you never know.

Land of plenty or land of want, where the grey Companions dance,
Feast or famine, or hope or fear, and in all things land of chance,
Where Nature pampers or Nature slays, in her ruthless red, romance.

And we catch a sound of a fairy's song, as the wind goes whipping by,
Or a scent like incense drifts along from the herbage ripe and dry
—Or the dust-storms dance on their ballroom floor,
where the bones of the cattle lie.

# Foreword

The big white English swan, escaped from captivity, found himself swimming in an Australian waterhole fringed with giant gumtrees. In one of the lower forks of a gumtree sat a placid round-eyed elderly gentleman apparently thinking of nothing whatever — in other words, a native bear.

"Excuse me, sir," said the swan, "can you tell me where I am?"

"Why, you're here," said the bear.

"I know I'm here," said the swan, thinking that his new acquaintance was dull-witted; "but where is 'here'? You see, I'm an English swan —"

"Excuse me," said the bear, "swans are black. I've seen thousands of 'em."

"They're black in this country," said the swan, "just the same as the aboriginals are black; but they are white in England, just the same as the people there are white. I don't like mentioning it, but our family are very highly regarded in England — one of the oldest families. We came to England from Cyprus with Richard Coeur-de-Lion."

"I'm a bit in that line myself," said the bear. "Did you ever hear of the Flood, when Noah took the animals in the Ark? Well, my people wouldn't go in the Ark. They didn't see any chance of getting fresh gumleaves every day, and they heard that this Noah was not too reliable. A capable chap — he must have been a capable chap to organise that outfit — but inclined to drink. So our people climbed trees and lived on gumleaves till the water went down. They say the Flood wasn't as high here as it was in other places, but I've never seen a flood yet but what somebody would tell you it was higher at his place than at yours. Have you any friends here?"

"I'm afraid not," said the swan, "but you never know. I'll give a call."

So he put up his head and sent a call echoing through the bush like the clang of a great brazen gong. Twice he repeated it, but no answer came.

"No luck," said the bear. "Anyone within two miles would be deaf if he didn't hear that. I'm pretty good, myself, at making people hear me. We got a lot of practice in the Flood, shouting to each other from the trees, and when we saw old Noah drifting on to a sandbank, we'd give him a hail. Listen to me."

And throwing his head back, he emitted the weirdest and most unmusical noise you ever heard. It sounded like an empty train running over an iron bridge.

"I could have had good money to go on the stage," he said, "but of course in my position I couldn't consider it. What would people think?"

"I suppose you have a lot of friends," said the swan.

"Well, not exactly friends," said the bear. "You see, we of the old families have to be a bit particular. We can't associate with these *nouveaux riches* and Johnny-come-lately people that you see about. Now, there's the 'possums—people that pretend to be relations of mine, but they're not. I saw one of them hanging upside down by the tail from a limb one night. Most undignified. Thank goodness, no matter what has happened to us, we have never grown tails. The Platypus family is as old as we are, but they live in the water, and I have never touched water, inside or outside, in my life; so we don't see anything of them."

"Do *they* date back to the Flood?" said the swan, who was thinking that after all Coeur-de-Lion seemed quite modern compared to these people.

"Oh, yes," said the bear. "They wouldn't go in the Ark either. Couldn't see any hope of getting their regular food, and there was a first-class chance of getting trodden on by the elephant. So they took to the water and they had the time of their lives. Plenty of food, and they drifted about on floating logs and fence-posts all day long. Didn't even have to swim. That was a gentleman's life, if you like."

"What is there up this creek?" said the swan. "Do you travel about much?"

"Me travel!" said the bear. "Do I look like it? Why should I? They say there are better trees up the creek, but what was good enough for my fathers is good enough for me. One of our people went wandering all over the place, half a mile up the creek, and he climbed a tree with a bee's nest in it and they stung him till his nose swelled up like an elephant's trunk. That's what he got for being one of these revolutionary chaps. Served him right."

"Well," said the swan, "I'm glad to have met you, and I think I'd better be moving on."

"Not a bit of it," said the bear, "not a bit of it. Never move on when you're lost. If people that are lost would sit still they'd be all right; but they will keep moving about and they die before people can catch up with them. Stay where you are and someone's sure to hear of you and they'll come here to look for you."

While they were talking, the surface of the waterhole below them was as smooth as glass. Then, without a splash or ripple, a lithe brown creature rose to the surface and drifted there soundlessly, looking up at them with bright little eyes.

"Good-day, Mr. Platypus," said the bear. "This," he went on, indicating the swan with a wave of his hand, "is an English friend of mine. I want you to take him where he can get a good feed of waterlily roots and frogs, and then fetch him back here. We'll boil the billy and make a night of it. He can tell us about Richard Coeur-de-Lion, and we can tell him about these neighbours of ours."

And it is from what the native bear and the platypus said that night that this book is written.

A. B. PATERSON

# Frogs in Chorus

The chorus frogs in the big lagoon
Would sing their songs to the silvery moon.
Tenor singers were out of place,
For every frog was a double bass.
But never a human chorus yet
Could beat the accurate time they set.
The solo singer began with the joke;
He sang "As long as I live I'll croak,
        Croak, I'll croak,"
And the chorus followed him: "Croak, croak, croak!"

The poet frog, in his plaintive tone,
Sang of a sorrow was all his own;
"How shall I win to my heart's desire?
How shall I feed my spirit's fire?"
And the solo frog in his deepest croak,
"To fire your spirit," he sang, "eat coke,
    Coke, eat coke,"
And the chorus followed him: "Coke, coke, coke!"

The green frog sat in a swampy spot
And he sang the song of he knew not what.
"The world is rotten, oh cursed spite,
That I am the frog that must set it right.
How shall I scatter the shades that lurk?"
And the old-man bull-frog sang "Get work,
    Work, get work,"
And the chorus followed him: "Work, work, work!"

The soaring spirits that fain would fly
On wings of hope to the starry sky
Must face the snarls of the jealous dogs,
For the world is ruled by its chorus frogs.

# High Explosive

'Twas the dingo pup to his dam that said
"It's time I worked for my daily bread.
Out in the world I intend to go,
And you'd be surprised at the things I know.

"There's a wild duck's nest in a sheltered spot,
And I'll go right down and I'll eat the lot."
But when he got to his destined prey
He found that the ducks had flown away.

But an egg was left
  that would quench
  his thirst,
So he bit the egg
  and it straightway
  burst.

It burst with a bang, and he turned and fled,
For he thought that the egg had shot him dead.

"Oh, mother," he said, "let us clear right out
Or we'll lose our lives with the bombs about;
And it's lucky I am that I'm not blown up —
It's a very hard life," said the dingo pup.

# Weary Will

The strongest creature for his size
But least equipped for combat
That dwells beneath Australian skies
Is Weary Will the Wombat.

He digs his homestead underground,
He's neither shrewd nor clever;
For kangaroos can leap and bound
But wombats dig for ever.

The boundary-rider's netting fence
Excites his irritation;
It is to his untutored sense
His pet abomination.

And when to pass it he desires,
Upon his task he'll centre
And dig a hole beneath the wires
Through which the dingoes enter.

And when to block the hole they strain
With logs and stones and rubble,
Bill Wombat digs it out again
Without the slightest trouble.

The boundary-rider bows to fate,
Admits he's made a blunder,
And rigs a little swinging gate
To let Bill Wombat under.

So most contentedly he goes
Between his haunt and burrow:
He does the only thing he knows,
And does it very thorough.

# The Diggers

*Bristling Billy the porcupine,*
*A person that nobody liked,*
*Sinking a shaft on an ant-bed mine,*
*Came on a burrowing lizard's line,*
*And the lizard was badly spiked.*
*"You're a blundering fool," said the snake's half-brother —*
*And that was how one thing led to another.*


Weary Willie the wombat king
Said he was champion excavator;
But the Bristler said "You ain't no such thing;
You couldn't dig up a new pertater!"
So a match was made on their mining skill —
Bristling Bill and Weary Will.

Both of the creatures were stout as steel,
With knife-like claws that could dig for ever.
The wombat dug with the greater zeal,
But he hadn't the style or the action clever
Of Bristling Billy, who looked a winner
Till he struck some ants, and he stopped for dinner.

Down where the ants had hid their young
Underground in a secret tunnel,
Scooping them up with his sticky tongue
Into his mouth that was like a funnel:
"Why should I dig for your wagers scanty,"
Said he, "When I'm feeling so fall and ant-y?"

A kangaroo who had lost his cash
Was wild at this most absurd come-uppance.
"Now listen, you poor ant-eating trash,
I'd give you a kick in the ribs for twopence!"
"Well, when I've finished with this here diet,"
Said Bristling Billy, "You come and try it."

*Bristling Billy the porcupine,*
*A person that nobody likes,*
*Wanders away on his lonely line,*
*Rattles his fearful spikes.*
*Says he, "There's none of you long-haired squibs*
*Is game to give me a kick in the ribs."*

# Old Man Platypus

Far from the trouble and toil of town,
Where the reed-beds sweep and shiver,
Look at a fragment of velvet brown —
Old Man Platypus drifting down,
Drifting along the river.

And he plays and dives in the river bends
In a style that is most elusive;
With few relations and fewer friends,
For Old Man Platypus descends
From a family most exclusive.

He shares his burrow beneath the bank
With his wife and his son and daughter
At the roots of the reeds and the grasses rank;
And the bubbles show where our hero sank
To its entrance under water.

Safe in their burrow below the falls
They live in a world of wonder,
Where no one visits and no one calls,
They sleep like little brown billiard balls
With their beaks tucked neatly under.

And he talks in a deep unfriendly growl
As he goes on his journey lonely;
For he's no relation to fish nor fowl,
Nor to bird nor beast, nor to horned owl;
In fact, he's the one and only!

# Flying Squirrels

On the rugged water-shed
At the top of the bridle track
Where years ago, as the old men say,
The splitters went with a bullock-dray
But never a dray came back;


At the time of the gumtree bloom,
When the scent in the air is strong,
And the blossom stirs in the evening breeze,
You may see the squirrels among the trees,
Playing the whole night long.


Never a care at all
Bothers their simple brains;
You can see them glide in the moonlight dim
From tree to tree and from limb to limb,
Little grey aeroplanes.

Each like a dormouse sleeps
In the spout of a gumtree old,
A ball of fur with a silver coat;
Each with his tail around his throat
For fear of his catching cold.

These are the things he eats,
Asking his friends to dine:
Moths and beetles and new-born shoots,
Honey and snacks of the native fruits,
And a glass of dew for wine.

# Fur and Feathers

The emus formed a football team
Up Walgett way;
Their dark-brown sweaters were a dream
But kangaroos would sit and scream
To watch them play.


"Now, butter-fingers," they would call,
And such-like names;
The emus couldn't hold the ball
— They had no hands — but hands aren't all
In football games.


A match against the kangaroos
They played one day.
The kangaroos were forced to choose
Some wallabies and wallaroos
That played in grey.

The rules that in the West prevail
Would shock the town;
For when a kangaroo set sail
An emu jumped upon his tail
And fetched him down.

A whistler duck as referee
Was not admired.
He whistled so incessantly
The teams rebelled, and up a tree
He soon retired.

The old marsupial captain said
"It's do or die!"
So down the ground like fire he fled
And leaped above an emu's head
And scored a try.

Then shouting "Keep it on the toes!"
The emus came.
Fierce as the flooded Bogan flows
They laid their foemen out in rows
And saved the game.

On native pear and Darling pea
They dined that night:
But one man was
    an absentee:
The whistler duck
    — their referee —
Had taken flight.

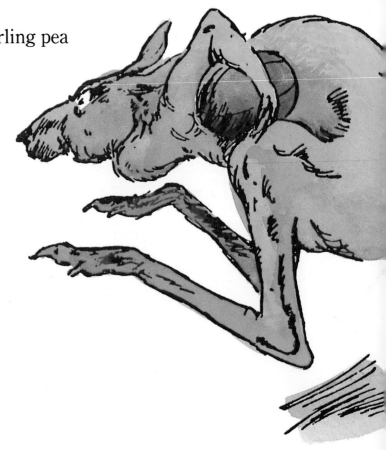

# Benjamin Bandicoot

If you walk in the bush at night,
In the wonderful silence deep,
By the flickering lantern light
When the birds are all asleep
You may catch sight of old Skinny-go-root,
Otherwise Benjamin Bandicoot.

With a snout that can delve and dig,
With claws that are as strong as steel,
He roots like a pigmy pig
To get his evening meal,
For creeping creatures and worms and roots
Are highly relished by bandicoots.

Under the grass and the fern
He fashions his beaten track
With many a twist and turn
That wanders and doubles back,
And dogs that think they are most astute
Are baffled by Benjamin Bandicoot.

In the depth of the darkest night,
Without a star in the sky,
He'll come to look at a light,
And scientists wonder why:
If the bush is burning
   it's time to scoot
Is the notion of
   Benjamin Bandicoot.

# A Bush Lawyer

When Ironbark the turtle came to Anthony's lagoon
The hills were hid behind a mist of equinoctial rain,
The ripple of the rivulets was like a cheerful tune
And wild companions waltzed among the grass as tall as grain.


But Ironbark the turtle cared no whit for all of these;
The ripple of the rivulets, the rustle of the trees
    Were only apple-sauce to him, or just a piece of cheese.


Now, Dan-di-dan the water-rat was exquisitely dressed,
For not a seal in Bass's Straits had half as fine a coat,
And every day he combed and brushed his golden-yellow vest,
A contrast with the white cravat he wore beneath his throat.

And Dan-di-dan the water-rat could move with ease and grace,
So Ironbark appeared to him a creature out of place,
  With iron-plated overcoat and dirty little face.

A crawfish at the point of death came drifting down the drains.
Said he: "I'm scalded to the heart with bathing near the bore."
The turtle and the water-rat disputed his remains,
For crawfish meat all day they'd eat, and then they'd ask for more.

Said Dan-di-dan: "The prize is mine, for I was fishing here
Before you tumbled down the bank and landed on your ear."
    "I wouldn't care," the turtle said, "if you'd have fished a year."

So Baggy-beak the Pelican was asked to arbitrate;
The scales of justice seemed to hang beneath his noble beak.
He said: "I'll take possession of the subject of debate";
He stowed the fish inside his pouch and then began to speak.

"The case is far from clear," he said, "and justices of note" —
But here he snapped his beak and flapped his piebald overcoat —
    "Oh dear," he said, "that wretched fish has slithered
        down my throat."


"But still," he said, "the point involved requires a full debate.
I'll have to get the lawyer-birds and fix a special day.
*Ad interim* I rule that costs come out of the estate."
And Baggy-beak the Pelican got up and flew away.


So both the pair who went to law were feeling very small.
Said they: "We might have halved the fish and saved a
        nasty brawl;
For half a crawfish isn't much, but more than none at all."

# Why the Jackass Laughs

The Boastful Crow and the Laughing Jack
Were telling tales of the outer back:
"I've just been travelling far and wide,
At the back of Bourke and the Queensland side;
There isn't a bird in the bush can go
As far as me," said the old black crow.

"There isn't a bird in the bush can fly
A course as straight or a course as high.
Higher than human eyesight goes
There's sometimes cloud — but there's always crows,
Drifting along for scent of blood
Or a smell of smoke or a sign of flood.

For never a bird or beast has been
With a sight as strong or a scent as keen.
At fires and floods I'm the first about,
For then the lizards and mice run out:
And I make my swoop — and that's all they know —
I'm a whale on mice," said the Boastful Crow.

The Bee-birds over the homestead flew
And told each other the long day through
"The cold has come, we must take the track."
"Now, I'll make you a bet," said the Laughing Jack,
"Of a hundred mice, that you dare not go
With the little Bee-birds, my Boastful Crow."

Said the Boastful Crow: "I could take my ease
And fly with little green birds like these.
If they went flat out and they did their best
I could have a smoke and could take a rest."
And he asked of the Bee-birds circling round:
"Now, where do you spike-tails think you're bound?"
"We leave to-night, and our present plan
Is to go straight on till we reach Japan.

"Every year, on the self-same day,
We call our children and start away,
Twittering, travelling day and night,
Over the ocean we take our flight;
And we rest a day on some lonely isles
Or we beg a ride for a hundred miles
On a steamer's deck,* and away we go:
We hope you'll come with us, Mister Crow."

But the old black crow was extremely sad.
Said he: "I reckon you're raving mad
To talk of travelling night and day,
And how in the world do you find your way?"
And the Bee-birds answered him: "If you please,
That's one of our own great mysteries."

Now, these things chanced in the long ago
And explain the fact, which no doubt you know,
That every jackass high and low
Will always laugh when he sees a crow.

*NOTE. — The writer has seen Eastern steamers green with the migrating bee-eaters.

# Camouflage

Beside the bare and beaten track of travelling flocks and herds
The woodpecker went tapping on, the postman of the birds:
"I've got a letter here," he said, "that no one's understood,
Addressed as follows: 'To the bird that's like a piece of wood.'

"The soldier-bird got very cross — it wasn't meant for her;
The spur-wing plover had a try to stab me with a spur:
The jackass laughed, and said the thing was written for a lark.
I think I'll chuck this postman job and take to stripping bark."

Then all the birds for miles around came in to lend a hand;
They perched upon a broken limb as thick as they could stand,
And just as old man eaglehawk prepared to have his say
A portion of the broken limb got up and flew away.

Then casting grammar to the winds, the postman said: "That's him!
The boo-book owl — he squats himself along a broken limb,
And pokes his beak up like a stick; there's not a bird, I vow,
Can tell you which is boo-book owl and which is broken bough.

"And that's the thing he calls his nest — that jerry-built affair —
A bunch of sticks across a fork; I'll leave his letter there.
A cuckoo wouldn't use his nest, but what's the odds to him —
A bird that tries to imitate a piece of leaning limb!"

# An Emu Hunt

West of Dubbo the West begins
The land of leisure and hope and trust,
Where the black man stalks with his dogs and gins
And Nature visits the settlers' sins
With the Bogan shower, that is mostly dust.


When the roley-poley's roots dry out
With the fierce hot winds and the want of rain.
They come uprooted and bound about
And dance in a wild fantastic rout
Like flying haystacks across the plain.


And the horses shudder and snort and shift
As the bounding mass of weed goes past,
But the emus never their heads uplift
As they look for roots in the sandy drift,
For the emus know it from first to last.

Now, the boss's dog that had come from town
Was strange to the wild and woolly West,
And he thought he would earn him some great renown
When he saw, on the wastes of the open down,
An emu standing beside her nest.

And he said to himself as he stalked his prey
To start on his first great emu hunt:
"I must show some speed when she runs away,
For emus kick very hard, they say;
But I can't be kicked if I keep in front."

The emu chickens made haste to flee
As he barked and he snarled and he darted round,
But the emu looked at him scornfully
And put an end to his warlike glee
With a kick that lifted him off the ground.


And when, with an injured rib or two,
He made for home with a chastened mind,
An old dog told him: "I thought you knew
An emu kicks like a kangaroo,
And you can't get hurt — IF YOU KEEP BEHIND."

# White Cockatoos

Now the autumn maize is growing,
Now the corn-cob fills,
Where the Little River flowing
Winds among the hills.
Over mountain-peaks outlying
Clear against the blue
Comes a scout in silence flying,
One white cockatoo.

Back he goes to where the meeting
Waits among the trees.
Says: "The corn is fit for eating;
Hurry, if you please."
Skirmishers, their line extending,
Shout the joyful news;
Down they drop like snow descending,
Clouds of cockatoos.

At their husking competition
Hear them screech and yell.
On a gumtree's high position
Sits a sentinel.
Soon the boss goes boundary-riding;
But the wise old bird,
Mute among the branches hiding,
Never says a word.

Then you hear his strident squalling:
"Here's the boss's son,
Through the garden bushes crawling,
Crawling with a gun.
May the spiny cactus bristles
Fill his soul with woe:
May his knees get full of thistles.
Brothers, let us go."

Old Black Harry sees them going,
Sketches Nature's plan:
"That one cocky too much knowing,
All same Chinaman.

One eye shut and one eye winkin' —
Never shut the two;
Chinaman go dead, me thinkin',
Jump up cockatoo."

# Buffalo Country

Out where the grey streams glide,
Sullen and deep and slow,
And the alligators slide
From the mud to the depths below
Or drift on the stream like a floating death,
Where the fever comes on the South wind's breath,
There is the buffalo.

Out on the big lagoons,
Where the Regia lilies float,
And the Nankin heron croons
With a deep ill-omened note,
In the ooze and the mud of the swamps below
Lazily wallows the buffalo,
Buried to nose and throat.


From the hunter's gun he hides
In the jungles dark and damp,
Where the slinking dingo glides
And the flying foxes camp;
Hanging like myriad fiends in line
Where the trailing creepers twist and twine
And the sun is a sluggish lamp.

On the edge of the rolling plains
Where the coarse cane grasses swell,
Lush with the tropic rains
In the noon-tide's drowsy spell,
Slowly the buffalo grazes through
Where the brolgas dance, and the jabiru
Stands like a sentinel.


All that the world can know
Of the wild and the weird is here,
Where the black men come and go
With their boomerang and spear,
And the wild duck darken the evening sky
As they fly to their nests in the reedbeds high
When the tropic night is near.

# A Dog's Mistake

### IN DOGGEREL VERSE

He had drifted in among us as a straw drifts with the tide,
He was just a wand'ring mongrel from the weary world
    outside;
He was not aristocratic, being mostly ribs and hair,
With a hint of spaniel parents and a touch of native bear.

He was very poor and humble and content with what he
    got,
So we fed him bones and biscuits, till he heartened up a lot;
Then he growled and grew aggressive, treating orders with
    disdain,
Till at last he bit the butcher, which would argue want of
    brain.

Now the butcher, noble fellow, was a sport beyond belief,
And instead of bringing actions he brought half a shin of
    beef,
Which he handed on to Fido, who received it as a right
And removed it to the garden, where he buried it at night.

'Twas the means of his undoing, for my wife, who'd stood
    his friend,
To adopt a slang expression, "went in off the deepest end,"
For among the pinks and pansies, the gloxinias and the
    gorse
He had made an excavation like a graveyard for a horse.

Then we held a consultation which decided on his fate:
'Twas in anger more than sorrow that we led him to the
    gate,
And we handed him the beef-bone as provision for the day,
Then we opened wide the portal and we told him "On your
    way."

# Black Harry's Team

No soft-skinned Durham steers are they,
No Devons plump and red,
But brindled, black, and iron-grey
That mark the mountain-bred;
For mountain-bred and mountain broke,
With sullen eyes agleam,
No stranger's hand could put a yoke
On old Black Harry's team.

Pull out, pull out, at break of morn
The creeks are running white,
And Tiger, Spot, and Snailey-horn
Must bend their bows by night;
And axles, wheels and flooring-boards
Are swept with flying spray
As, shoulder-deep, through mountain fords
The leaders feel their way.

He needs no sign of cross or kirn
To guide him as he goes,
For every twist and every turn
That old black leader knows.
Up mountains steep they heave and strain

Where never wheel has rolled,
And what the toiling leaders gain
The body-bullocks hold.

Where eaglehawks their eyries make,
On sidelings steep and blind,
He rigs the good old-fashioned brake —
A tree tied on behind.
Up mountains, straining to the full,
Each poler plays his part —
The sullen, stubborn, bullock-pull
That breaks a horse's heart.

Beyond the furthest bridle track
His wheels have blazed the way;
The forest giants, burnt and black,
Are ear-marked by his dray.
Through belts of scrub where messmates grow
His juggernaut has rolled,
For stumps and saplings have to go
When Harry's team takes hold.

On easy grade and rubber tyre
The tourist car goes through;
They halt a moment to admire
The far-flung mountain view.
The tourist folk would be amazed
If they could get to know
THEY TAKE THE TRACK BLACK HARRY BLAZED
A HUNDRED YEARS AGO.

# The Billy-Goat Overland

Come all ye lads of the droving days, ye gentlemen
    unafraid,
I'll tell you all of the greatest trip that ever a drover made,
For we rolled our swags, and we packed our bags, and
    taking our lives in hand,
We started away with a thousand goats, on the billy-goat
    overland.

There wasn't a fence that'd hold the mob, or keep 'em from
    their desires;
They skipped along the top of the posts and cake-walked on
    the wires.
And where the lanes had been stripped of grass and the
    paddocks were nice and green,
The goats they travelled outside the lanes and we rode in
    between.

The squatters started to drive them back, but that was no
    good at all,

Their horses ran for the lick of their lives from the scent
    that was like a wall:
And never a dog had pluck or gall in front of the mob to
    stand
And face the charge of a thousand goats on the billy-goat
    overland.

We found we were hundreds over strength when we
    counted out the mob;
And they put us in jail for a crowd of thieves that travelled
    to steal and rob:
For every goat between here and Bourke, when he scented
    our spicy band,
Had left his home and his work to join in the billy-goat
    overland.

# A.B. "BANJO" PATERSON

Andrew Barton Paterson was born on 17 February 1864 near Orange in New South Wales. As a young boy he spent many enjoyable hours exploring the Australian bush, discovering the extraordinary array of native birds and animals. It is from these early memories that Paterson created characters for his book of verses for children, *The Animals Noah Forgot*.

After leaving school, Paterson studied law in Sydney, while still enjoying visits to the bush. He was also involved in many sports, including tennis, polo, rowing and, in particular, horse racing, in which he achieved considerable success as an amateur jockey. Paterson still found time to write, however, and his verses began to be published in the *Bulletin* magazine under the pen-name of "Banjo" (a name Paterson took from a racehorse owned by his family).

Banjo Paterson is perhaps best known for poems like "The Man From Snowy River", which captured the flavour of both the Australian bush itself and the hardiness and humour of its people. But in *The Animals Noah Forgot* the poet turned his attention to the creatures of the bush, and found in their unique habits and appearance ample inspiration for a series of lively and amusing verses that have been delighting adults and children alike for over fifty years.

After a long and distinguished career as a journalist, war correspondent and the most popular balladist in Australia's literary history, Banjo Paterson died in 1941, shortly before his seventy-seventh birthday.

# NORMAN LINDSAY

Norman Lindsay was born in 1879 at Creswick in Victoria. He started drawing at a very early age and his natural talent was developed by an unfortunate childhood illness which kept him from playing but gave him lots of time to practise drawing.

Despite having had no formal art lessons, Lindsay mastered a wide variety of artistic techniques, and developed a formidable reputation for his black and white cartoons, his etchings, his paintings and his sculpture. He also turned his hand to writing, and had several comic novels published.

In 1918, his classic children's story, *The Magic Pudding*, appeared, to instant acclaim. One of the most popular Australian children's books ever written, it has been constantly in print for over seventy years and is still loved by children today. The liveliness and wit that make Lindsay's illustrations for *The Magic Pudding* so appealing can also be seen in the drawings he prepared for *The Animals Noah Forgot*, their light-heartedness perfectly complementing A. B. Paterson's verse.

The most famous member of a remarkably talented Australian family, Norman Lindsay died in 1969 at the grand old age of ninety.